The Fooditor

Where to eat
(and what to eat there)
in Chicago

Text and photos by
Michael Gebert
for Fooditor.com

for my 3 most frequent dining companions, S., M. and L.

ISBN: 978-1539913481

& Cream	3.25	Cold Cut Plate	11.95	Smoked Fish Plate	13
BERRIES	3.25	Tuna "	10.95	Sardine "	
aw	1.95	Salmon Salad Plate	10.95	Fruit "	
& Fruit	3.95	Salmon Plate	10.95	Lox Platter	
Chop Suey	6.50	Egg Salad "	10.95	Julienne Salad	

Introduction: 99 pleasures

There are two kinds of dining guides—there's the three-star kind, which imagines it's passing judgements engraved in stone for all time. And then there's the What's Hot To Eat Now!!! kind, that's about going to (and being seen at) the newest places.

Here's a third kind, and I think it's the kind that's most like asking someone who knows for some suggestions of where to go now. Parts of this guide point you to classic places, parts of it to exciting new ones, but the reason they're all in here is pleasure. Pleasure is the one thing you can always trust—you can fool yourself that some place is hot, that the chef is important, that ** was worth $$$$, but you know if it was delicious. You can't kid yourself that it made you go "Wow" if it didn't.

So here are 99 pleasures from all over the city. 99 restaurants that do something special, together with the info that will help you get the most from them—dishes to order, insight into what they're about, even a few secret menu items.

SANDWICHES
WARM

				DINNERS	SANDW
Salami	795	Turkey	11 95	HOT...	
Chopped Liver	795	Hamburger	6 95	Roast Beef	
American Cheese	495	Liver	8 95	Corned Beef	14
Swiss	,,	,, Tongue	11.95	Pastrami	9 5
Cream	,,	250 Frankwurst		Tongue	12.95
				Brisket	14 95

COFFEE

It's *not* a best restaurants list, in order from 1 to 99. "The 99 most exciting restaurants right now" comes closer to it, but even then there are fascinating and worthy places that are left off because they already get plenty of attention—starting with the two restaurants that got 3 stars from the French tire company. (If all the other guides have them, do you really need to see them here, too?) Instead, the point of this list is to try to convey a picture of the city as a whole, in all its edible diversity and creativity.

A few notes on how the sausage gets made: it's true that as a journalist rather than a reviewer, I'm not anonymous (to the extent anyone is). I do get invited to preview dinners and stuff like that, though to fewer places in here than you might think (none of the top ten, for instance, though a couple invited me to their anniversary parties). I've only written about places I've been to pretty recently, and have firm memories of and opinions on. Mainly, I've tried to be honest in my enthusiasm—and I hope you'll find some reasons to share it in here.

Michael Gebert

1. Fat Rice

Logan Square • Chinese, Brunch • $$
2957 W. Diversey, Chicago 773-661-9170

Simultaneously a hipster hangout, a culinary world of wonders and a scholarly examination of a little-known cuisine, the Portuguese-Chinese fusion cuisine of Macau (which they admit sometimes they're just making up), Fat Rice defines the creativity of the moment in Chicago with its informal setting, bright and earthy flavors—and expansion into things beyond dinner with dim sum, a Chinese bakery and a slinky bar (The Ladies' Room). *What to have:* The best things combine the bright spices of Asia with European traditions of funky cured meats and braising, for dishes with both heat and slow-cooking depth— like the smoky-hot piri piri chicken with its slow-burning heat, or the hearty arroz con gordo (aka fat rice), or balichang, sweet and sour pork belly with tart tamarind. But leave room for the funky fusion of desserts (which overlap with The Bakery's offerings) such as Portuguese egg tarts, or the Rice Krispy treat topped with pork floss and a fish sauce caramel for dipping.

Adrienne Lo of Fat Rice making dim sum

2. Birrieria Zaragoza

Archer Heights • Mexican • $
4852 S. Pulaski, Chicago 773-523-3700

Mexican food is central to Chicago, and this is
pretty much the city's most perfect Mexican family
restaurant—tender roasted birria, goat, served in a
deeply meaty consomme with fresh homemade tortillas
as chewy and satisfying as a Neapolitan pizza crust,
made by a friendly family in an old diner location.
What to order: goat consommé with housemade salsa;
quesadillas.

3. Giant

Logan Square • Contemporary, Small Plates • $$
3209 W. Armitage, Chicago 773-252-0997

Jason Vincent came to fame and Food + Wine Best New
Chef status for the hearty porkiness of Nightwood, so
it's a bit surprising that at Giant, he and co-chef Ben
Lustbader focus so much on vegetables. Not that it's
setting out to be a veggie place for any doctrinal reason,
you see the same complexity on meat dishes like the
baby back ribs, but vegetables are the perfect, not too
dominant foils for the complex and well-balanced flavors
of dishes like the roasted broccoli with hummus or the
dazzling eggplant with its complex Chinese-sweet-and-
sour-meets-steak-sauce glaze. Not far behind them are
the few, relatively simple but well-focused pasta dishes.
What to order: fried uni shooter, biscuit, sweet and sour
eggplant and whatever other vegetables look good,
sortallini and tajarin pastas.

4. Oriole

West Loop, Near West Side • Fine Dining, Tasting Menu • $$$$
661 W. Walnut, Chicago 312-877-5339

The exquisitely expensive and precious tasting menu has joined architecture and the blues as one of Chicago's great art forms, so how do you pick one among them? Set aside concerns over absolute standards, and just say which one is the most fun to dine at right now, and it's easily Oriole, not only because the food is so winning with its inventive-but-not-weird approach to luxe ingredients, but because the newest kid on that block is so genuine and genuinely welcoming, sweet and full of youthful enthusiasm.

Dishes like Alaskan king crab under coconut cream dotted with blackberries, or oysters set off with jamon iberico broth and lime, seem somehow comfortable and novel at the same time; even a slice of buttered bread baked in house makes a case for being one of the best things you've eaten in ages. Besides sailing on good vibes all night, dinner here is extremely well paced: you end the meal feeling not like a dissipated Roman senator, but rooting for chef Noah Sandoval, his wife and manager Cara, pastry chef Genie Kwon and the rest of the young, confident staff. *What to order:* tasting menu, they got this.

5. Boka

Lincoln Park • Contemporary, American • $$$
1729 N. Halsted, Chicago 312-337-6070

The Boka Group's original restaurant reinvented itself with the arrival of chef Lee Wolen, who'd once lived across the street but came to it by way of Eleven Madison Park in New York. Wolen basically set out to make arty tasting menu food in normal plate quantities, and that philosophy of delivering superior execution while taking a couple of steps back from preciousness pervades the entire restaurant, which has a clubby comfortableness (and a wall of quirky pictures embedded in moss in its patio room). *What to order:* Wolen made his name doing roast chicken, and it's fine in whatever form it takes now, but his Asian-tinged octopus dishes are always strong, and no table should be without a plate of the roasted carrots.

6. Snaggletooth

Lakeview • Seafood, Deli, Breakfast • $$

2819 N. Southport, Chicago 773-899-4711

Bill Montagne, a Chicago chef by way of Le Bernardin in New York, and Jennifer Kim (a winner of the S. Pellegrino Almost Famous Chef Competition who worked at Ruxbin), met like DiCaprio and Winslet in the Titanic of a big opening (C Chicago, now Ocean Cut). They came away from it with just one thing that got good reviews, housecured fish—and on their own they opened a little miracle of a place devoted to that alone. Today their refrigerator is stuffed with salmon, trout and other fish in the process of curing, which they serve on crusty bread or butter-grilled bagels with light-tasting yogurt-based schmears. It's like Jewish deli sushi, the delicate beauty of pristine seafood in unpretentious, grab-a-cup-of-coffee (Sparrow) and-read-the-newspaper form. *What to order:* cured fish plate, O.G. bagel and lox, whitefish toast.

7. Smyth & The Loyalist

West Loop • Fine Dining, Tasting Menu, Farm To Table • Smyth: $$$$ Loyalist: $$
177 N. Ada, Chicago 773-913-3772

Smyth is the tasting menu upstairs, and I had one thing there—an anise-tasting cured egg dessert—that ranked among the best, most mind-boggling foods of my life. But on the way to that was a mix of highs and hmms, leaving me convinced that chefs John and Karen Shields are working toward something new and great in their playing with briny Asian flavors and umami-rich concoctions like marmite—but for me, it is a work in progress. The restaurant itself has a remarkably welcoming air, like chefs set up in one corner of *your* living room, and you may well want to check it out for the experience, which is top-notch.

On the other hand The Loyalist, the downstairs lounge and bar, is a plain black basement—yet it was love at first bite for the simple, astonishingly precise flavors here, clearly in the footsteps of Charlie Trotter (but at far more reasonable prices). Set aside the burger (with bacon ground into it and a marmite spread, it tastes like a BBQ burger) that's gotten all the press, because the simplest dishes here are the best—things like canteloupe dusted with spices and lime leaf, or a salad of fresh and roasted tomatoes with cheese, or a Southern biscuit served with butter mixed with spicy nduja sausage. *What to order:* Smyth: tasting menu. The Loyalist: biscuit; secret menu item of chicken with liver mousse gravy; whatever looks seasonal and unusual; toasted pavlova for dessert.

8. Hanbun

Westmont • Korean, Tasting Menu • $/$$$
665 Pasquinelli Dr., Westmont 630-948-3383

Dave Park spent time at L2O, Tru and other spots
like that, which you can see even in the fairly modest
but expertly flavored and prepared Korean lunchtime
offerings at this stand in a Westmont Asian mall food
court; if life puts you near these suburbs, do not miss
the chance to have lunch here. Where it really blossoms,
though, is with the juhnyuk (tasting menu) he offers pre-
arranged groups of six to eight, after hours in the mall.
The incongruity of dining in a Sbarro's-sized kitchen
quickly gives way to delight at the visual imaginativeness
(that's a dumpling dish of his on the cover) and subtlety of
his fine dining plates, which incorporate Korean flavors,
often fairly strong, while still reflecting the fine dining
refinement of his training. He's going to be a star—check
him out while his prices are still so reasonable. *What to
order:* at lunch, jjajjangmyun (noodles in black bean sauce),
spicy rice cakes, korean ramyun (chicken based ramen).

9. Vera

Near West Side, West Loop • Spanish, Small Plates, Wine Bar • $$$
1023 W. Lake, Chicago 312-243-9770

The comfortable, grownup wine bar Vera is ostensibly
Spanish, but I don't usually think of it that way—
there are relatively few of the standard dishes that are
seen in American takes on Spanish food (though yes,
there's paella on Wednesday and Sunday). Vera comes
closest to tapas bars in Spain where "Spanishness"
is less about specific seasonings or flavors and more
about a philosophy of simple, direct presentation of

great seasonal things; chef Mark Mendez seems to get suspicious if anything needs more than olive oil and a little salt or lemon, and his minimalism often yields maximum delights. But what it will need is a glass of sherry from his wife Liz. *What to order:* boquerones (fresh anchovies), grilled beef tongue, shrimp a la plancha, fabada (Thursday only).

10. Blackbird

Near West Side, West Loop • Contemporary, Farm to Table, Tasting Menu • $$$
619 W. Randolph, Chicago 312-715-0708

Blackbird has been arguably the biggest trendsetter of the last 20 years in Chicago, sending cooks, a love of bold and porky flavors, and the idea that restaurants should be minimalist, loud and lively all over town. Yet it's also been a changeling restaurant, reinventing itself with the chefs who have taken over as Paul Kahan oversees a growing empire. The current chef de cuisine, Ryan Pfeiffer, came up through David Posey's kitchen after some time in California, and there seems a bit of a Californian touch right now, with dishes that are very direct in their presentation of a few fresh flavors, usually plated all in the middle (so you have to taste everything together, he says). At first glance the plates seem delicately beautiful, but there's usually a surprise—a potato and kale soup has some chile heat, a sturgeon dish has, strangely, a sauce tasting of almond extract—and you realize Pfeiffer's flavor combinations are unusually bold as well as beautiful. This version of Blackbird is ready to go head to head with Grace, Boka or anybody in town. *What to order:* changes more or less monthly; there's a tasting menu, and one of the best deals in town is the $25 lunch.

11. Vie

Western Springs • American, Farm to Table • $$$
4471 Lawn Ave., Western Springs 708-246-2082

Not enough Chicagoans go to suburban Western Springs for Paul Virant's farm to table food (even though you could make a romantic getaway by train there), but it hardly seems to matter when you see a room full of snowy-haired suburbanites chomping down on deep porkiness and farm to table house-pickled vegetables as if they were Logan Square hipsters or something, man. I've only been a few times myself, but Vie holds a disproportionate place in best things I've ever eaten anyway. *What to order:* changes with the seasons, but honestly, you can't go wrong.

12. Arbor

Logan Square • Farm to Table, Tasting Menu, Breakfast • $$
2545 W. Diversey, Chicago 312-866-0795

Arbor is hidden on the second floor of a LEED-certified building full of internet startups, and what's unusual about it hardly stops there—it serves breakfast and lunch with a natural foods bent (including lots of things grown out back), plus a 3-night-a-week "Midwestern Omakase" tasting menu tailored to the guest via an email questionnaire. For dinner, the tasting menu is inventive and unusual, a fun and warm experience in which they'll happily chat with you at length about food or the eclectic wine choices. At lunch, the Harvest, a grilled cauliflower sandwich with rhubarb mostarda, has as much of the heartiness of a corned beef sandwich as any vegetarian alternative will ever have.

But for all that, I'd say Arbor's great meal is breakfast—mostly driven by grains and full of fresh ingredients, they've kind of spoiled me for standard issue breakfast plates, and so has the low-key experience of hanging out here in what just might be the future of restaurants and working. *What to order:* biscuit sandwiches, Toast and..., Midwest Grains for breakfast; Harvest at lunch; Midwestern omakase.

John Zaragoza of Birrieria Zaragoza

13. The Purple Pig

Near North Side • Italian, Small Plates • $$
500 N. Michigan, Chicago 312-464-1744

If anybody is visiting and staying downtown, this is my first recommendation. It's not just that the food is so good—though Jimmy Bannos Jr.'s kind of Italian (but almost no pasta), kind of Greek food *is* simple and incredibly delicious; I can reel off things I loved five years ago there, beets with thick Greek yogurt, manila clams in a spicy tomato broth, a comforting yogurt and farro dessert... It's a great advertisement for Chicago cooking, direct, Italian-tinged and unfussy. But it's also impressive how they handle the neverending stream of aspiring diners in such a tiny little place. They're the city restaurant that works—and wows. *What to order:* charcuterie is a big push, and pork is all over the menu, but don't overdo them—vegetable and seafood dishes have often been the things that impressed me the most.

14. 42 Grams

Uptown • Fine Dining, Tasting Menu • $$$$
4662 N. Broadway, Chicago

There was a lot of press recently about the first Singapore hawker stand to get a Michelin star. There ought to have been as much about 42 Grams winning two in its first year, because both demonstrate how much of fine dining's trappings you can actually do without and even win Michelin's approval. 42 Grams started as an underground restaurant in the apartment of chef Jake Bickelhaupt, who'd worked for Charlie Trotter and Alinea, and his wife Alexa. Now it's in the posher space below it, but the experience has hardly changed—luxe ingredients, combined and plated as well as anywhere in town for balance of flavors and visual appeal, served as personally as if you were in their dining room at home. (Not least because capacity is all of 8 or 10 at a time.) They prove that you can rival any restaurant as long as you have intensity and focus, a really good Trotter-refined palate—and, as Bickelhaupt pointed out to me in an interview in his underground dining days, a credit card to order the same level of ingredients "real" restaurants do. I can't speak to the credit card, but the others are obvious. *What to order:* tasting menu; BYO a couple of nice bottles of white wine.

15. Coalfire

West Town • Pizza • $$
1321 W Grand, Chicago 312-226-2625

Lakeview • Pizza • $$
3707 N. Southport, Chicago 773-477-2625

Popularly, Chicago is associated with deep dish pizza, numerically the bulk of it is thin crust pizza... but since Spacca Napoli appeared in the early 2000s, we've been a city chasing Neapolitan pizza perfection. And honestly, you can find letter-perfect Neapolitan pizzas in a number of places now—besides Spacca Napoli, Forno Rosso, Eataly, La Madia, and so on. Coalfire is, by that standard, a little imperfect—it's Neapolitan crossed with New Haven. A bubbly crust with delicious burnt spots, some tomato pies and some white pizzas, balanced on a can of tomatoes at your table—perfect imperfection. *What to order:* margherita, white pizza, 'nduja.

16. The Milk Room

The Loop • Cocktails • $$$$
12 S. Michigan, Chicago

The Chicago Athletic Association Hotel is an entry unto itself, full of nooks and crannies, and the nookest and cranniest of them all is this pocket bar tucked behind the reception desk on the lobby floor. Everything about it is so, so up to the minute in delivering a vintage experience: you book a two hour slot online. You enter the room, dark as a confessional, or an opium den. You consult with your mixologist over what you like. You may taste a few old time spirits   and though some would argue that spirits don't age like wine, many of them are things that aren't made the same way any more, so you're tasting Havana in the 50s. Finally, a drink is made for you, that may well cost $50 or more. Many will find that absurd. That's why it's magic—you've bought into an experience that only you can appreciate. There's a little food on the menu, also highly priced, but that's not why you're here. *What to order:* whatever your drink consultant and you decide.

17. The Bristol

Bucktown • American, Farm to Table • $$$
2152 N. Damen, Chicago 773-862-5555

Chris Pandel is back in the kitchen of his original restaurant, removing some things (fried rice is out) and reviving others (monkey bread is back). But those are minor details compared to The Bristol's longterm mission, the devotion to porkiness, offal, buying from farmers, housemade pasta and in general a lack of pretension in fine dining which made it one of the best and most influential restaurants in town. *What to order:* head-on prawns, papardelle bolognese, Amish half chicken, hanger steak, basque cake.

18. mfk

Lakeview • Seafood, Spanish • $$
432 W. Diversey, Chicago 773-857-2540

Step down into this small space and you'll feel like you've escaped to sunny Spain even when the snow is blowing outside. The menu takes an admirably direct approach to simple, mostly seafood dishes, and an equally direct one to modestly-priced, likable wines and welcoming service. That's all there is to say, except that I wish we had many more like it. *What to order:* boquerones, albondigas, octopus, basque cake.

19. Honey 1 BBQ

Grand Boulevard • Barbecue • $
746 E. 43rd, Chicago 773-285-9455

After struggling in Bucktown for several years, Honey 1 pitmaster Robert Adams moved to the south side, and he's never seemed happier than now with an appreciative crowd for his generously meaty cuts of Chicago barbecue, slow-cooked for maximum smoky flavor in an "aquarium" glass and steel pit. *What to order:* Rib tips, hot links, brisket. Take-out only.

20. Khan BBQ

West Rogers Park • Indian/Pakistani, Grill • $$
2401 W. Devon, Chicago 773-338-2800

Unlike the ubiquitous buffets on Devon, Khan BBQ cooks to order—not just *cooks*, but grills meat on skewers inside big concrete tandoors. The result is some of the best grilled meat in the city, electric with bright South Asian spices, like the raita-coated chicken boti or the Cheetos-orange goat chanp (chops). There are also comfier rice dishes like frontier chicken and lamb biryani, and you can fill out your feast very reasonably with vegetable stews and some naan or parantha, but your priority should be the things that come out of that magical tandoor. *What to order:* Chicken boti, goat chanp, broasted chicken, frontier chicken.

21. El Che Bar

West Loop • South American, Grill • $$$
845 W. Washington, Chicago 312-265-1130

Argentine grills are all over all of a sudden, but none has a more dramatic setting than the one at the far end of this sultry bar and restaurant, an inferno chefs John Manion and Mark Steuer tend like guys shoveling coal in a steamship. (They're talking about putting seats next to it, which I think means that they no longer realize how hot it is back there.) But they know what they're doing with it, too—from smoking scamorza cheese for a novel take on the ubiquitous beet salad, to South American-tinged meats ranging from steak to quail, they hit the precise spot between macho pyrotechnics and a swanky night out. *What to order:* roasted beets, lamb ribs, head-on prawns, charred quail; caramelized Old Fashioned.

22. Sumi Robata Bar

River North • Japanese • $$$
702 N. Wells, Chicago 312-988-7864

This small Japanese restaurant stands apart from others in town for its size (tiny and thus much more authentically sized than most) and the quiet perfectionism of chef Gene Kato. The menu includes some sashimi items, but don't stop there—you'll want some of the things grilled by hand over binchotan grills, as well as dishes like the creamy, chawanmushi-like tofu bowl with caviar, or the luxurious jidori kimo, chicken liver mousse. Make a separate reservation or ask about the small-capacity Charcoal Bar downstairs. *What to order:* dinner: tofu, smoked kamo, jidori kimo, ochazuke; any grilled items, including chicken heart and chicken oyster (limited quantities on both). Lunch: bento box.

23. Monteverde

West Loop • Italian • $$$
1020 W. Madison, Chicago 312-888-3041

Sarah Grueneberg was the chef of Spiaggia long enough that it's hard to imagine what she could do that differently in a new Italian restaurant—her own, with fellow graduate of Tony Mantuano's kitchens Meg Sahs. One thing was installing a big pasta-making station, visible at the bar; many of the pastas are made freshly here, some drying over the heads of patrons. Another was putting woks in the kitchen—and so the menu got divided into Pasta Tipica and Pasta Atipica, classic and modern. Either way, it's all handsomely made, eclectic enough to be novel, and happy eating in the comfortable, vaguely villa-like room, whether it's nice enough to open the French doors to the outside or not. *What to order:* nduja arancini, prosciutto butter toast, cacio whey pepe, tortelloni di zucca, ragu ala napoletana.

24. Hoosier Mama Pie Co.

West Town, Ukrainian Village • Bakery • $
1618-1/2 W. Chicago, Chicago 312-243-4846

Dollop Coffee & Hoosier Mama Pie Co.: Evanston • Bakery • $
749 Chicago, Evanston 847-868-8863

Once there was a dark time when many things were rare in Chicago. Others wished for ramen or Nashville hot chicken, but for me, it was pie. Why didn't diners serve pie here? Why was there only gloppy supermarket pie? Then Paula Haney, who'd worked at

Sarah Grueneberg of Monteverde

places like Alinea, started making real butter-crust pie while caring about seasonality and stuff like that. Now we live in a pie age, but the standard is still set by Hoosier Mama's two locations. *What to order:* apple pie, chess pie, Hoosier sugar cream pie; savory pork pie; pie, pie, pie!

25. The Publican

West Loop • Beer, American, Brunch • $$$
837 W. Fulton Market, Chicago 312-733-9555

Great beer list, loud place that looks like a modernist beer hall, lots of pork on the menu, a fair amount of really good seafood and vegetables on the menu, a fair amount of salt in everything that keeps you ordering beer, the most popular brunch in town, maybe not in numbers (that line at the Bongo Room is pretty long) but surely in zeitgeisty essentialness, service that varies a lot in attentiveness... The Publican is less a restaurant than a microcosm of Chicago, boisterous and flavorful and not for the easily discouraged. Love Chicago, love The Publican. *What to order:* oysters, roasted clams, barbecue carrots, Publican bread plate, Toulouse sausage, spicy pork rinds, ham chop in hay.

26. La Chaparrita

Little Village • Mexican • $
2500 S. Whipple, Chicago 773-254-0975

Though it's located a block from a busy taco strip on 26th, you'd probably never stumble on your own upon this Day of the Dead-themed taqueria tucked into the neighborhood (I didn't either; it was an LTHForum find years ago). Its strengths are earthy peasant cuts, and while you could order steak or chorizo here, you want to be bold and try things like longaniza (housemade sausage), lengua (tongue) and especially the crispy tripas, which are as delectable as bacon. *What to order:* Tacos. Don't be afraid of tripe.

27. Parachute

Avondale · Korean · $$$

3500 N. Elston, Chicago 773-654-1460

This was Beverly Kim (Charlie Trotter's, *Top Chef*) and her husband Johnny Clark's second attempt at launching an upscale Korean restaurant, and this time they found the sweet spot in a thrift-shop-funky place on a semi-dead strip of Elston. Though not quite as wide-ranging as Fat Rice's menu, the inventive offerings cover similar territory from delicate sashimi crudos, to funky east-west fusion dishes like the pork with figs and X.O., though authentically core Korean flavors (like gochujang hot sauce) dominate. *What to order:* bing bread for sure, otherwise make your own picks from the frequently changing menu.

28. 5 Loaves Eatery

Greater Grand Crossing · Breakfast, Soul Food, Chicken · $

405 E. 75th, Chicago 773-891-2889

Sweet and welcoming African-American family-run restaurant, serving some of the best fried chicken—I mean, top 3—in town, and other comfort foods like shrimp and grits. But the real comfort here is the bond they form with their customers, who are liable to get up to give them a hug at any moment. *What to order:* fried chicken, po' boy sandwich, shrimp and grits (weekends only), salmon croquettes, lemon poppyseed pancakes, anything that comes with a biscuit.

29. Publican Quality Meats

West Loop · Sandwiches, Deli, Breakfast · $$

825 W. Fulton Market, Chicago 312-445-8977

Insanely delicious sandwiches (plus a few things like a tripe-filled ribbolita stew) on crusty Publican bread, in a market/butcher shop (where you can also buy the same things they use). What more is there to say, except to thank chef Paul Kahan (Blackbird etc.) for never losing his deli roots and keeping this kind of deliciousness affordable? *What to order:* Parm #2, Return of the Gyro, ribollita, butcher's charcuterie plate.

30. Immm Rice & Beyond

Uptown • Thai • $
4949 N. Broadway, Chicago 773-293-7378

A cafeteria line in a Thai restaurant hardly seems a good sign, compared to how good freshly-made Thai food is, but there's a method here: the line focuses on dishes typically sold on the street premade in Thailand, so it constitutes a lot of things we haven't seen in Chicago Thai restaurants before. Add in that co-owner Dew Suriyawan (who ran Spoon Thai for a bit with his sisters) is willing to put things on the menu without fear of how funky or strong they are—a fact that you'll realize as soon as you open the door—and Immm counts as one of the most authentic and adventurous Thai restaurants, not just in Chicago, but probably in the U.S. Does strong and funky equal delicious? Well, yes, mostly, if you've had experience with Thai food already and are used to the Thai palette of flavors. In any case, they're willing to guide you and the three for $11 lunch special reduces your risk. *What to order:* paa lo (pork belly with hardboiled egg), khanom jeen nam ya (curry with fish balls), panang curry, khao moo dang (barbecue pork).

31. Leña Brava

West Loop, Near West Side • Mexican, Seafood • $$$
900-902 W. Randolph, Chicago 312-733-1975

Whatever else you get, get the whole striped bass. Butterflied and grilled perfectly over live fire with one of four possible Mexican marinades, it completely justifies Rick Bayless's attempt to create a Baja beachside seafood grill in the West Loop. Sample from the rest of the menu—the aguachiles (basically crudos) are good, the laminados (think Mexican sashimi) seemed less convincing at selling the idea that earthy Mexican flavors set off pristine fish as well as Asian or Mediterranean ones. *What to order:* Striped bass, black cod "al pastor," pineapple aguachile, cauliflower mash.

32. Elizabeth

Lincoln Square • Fine Dining, Tasting Menu • $$$
4835 N. Western, Chicago 773-681-0651

Iliana Regan was one of a kind when she turned up running her own restaurant, built on foraged ingredients, her experience mainly as an underground chef—and her indomitable will about what she wanted to make. Those early days seemed to have a lot to prove, and though menus with vegetables and leaves picked from wild corners of the area plus the occasional protein like raccoon were fascinating as all get out, they could be a little austere. My most recent meal showed that she's arrived at a place where dinner is lusher and more obviously pleasurable while still looking at the world from an angle no one else quite does, making "fascinating" an easier sell without compromising her own sense of starkly honest food deeply rooted in what grows, often wild, in the midwest. *What to order:* tasting menu.

33. Red Hot Ranch

Lakeview • Burgers, Hot Dogs • $
3057 N. Ashland, Chicago 773-661-9377

Vienna Beef dogs served Chicago-style as they should be, mustard, onion, relish and rolled up with fresh cut fries so the potatoes pick up the taste of mustard and onion. Burgers served with a suspicious resemblance to In'N'Out style... and dare I say they make a better smashed burger than that California legend? I dare. *What to order:* Red Hot Ranch Burger, hot dog.

34. Table, Donkey & Stick

Logan Square • European, Wine Bar • $$
2728 W. Armitage, Chicago 773-486-8525

A chill neighborhood restaurant with a theme loosely inspired by Alpine cuisine, Table, Donkey & Stick has three advantages (none of which are the mouthful of a name): the mellow farm to table food of chef Scott Manley, graduate of Blackbird and Vie, who's a bit of a mad scientist when it comes to the housemade charcuterie, working in oddball ingredients; the crusty bread that co-owner Matt Sussman is very proud of making; and the reasonable and eclectic wine program (the Tuesday night producer tastings are one of the best wine deals in town). *What to order:* Charcuterie, house bread, rabbit crepinette, duck sausage, Alpine burger.

35. Nha Hang Viet Nam

Uptown • Vietnamese • $
1032 W. Argyle, Chicago 773-878-8895

Most non-Vietnamese visiting Argyle Street don't look much beyond pho, but for a fuller range of Vietnamese cuisine visit this family run spot with pretty minimal English but a James Brown-level vocabulary of spicy funk. *What to order:* rare beef salad, woven rice cake with pork, clay pot pork and catfish, bun mam, spicy crabs.

36. Smoque

Irving Park • Barbecue • $$
3800 N. Pulaski, Chicago 773-545-7427

The Loop • Barbecue • $$
Revival Food Hall, 125 S. Clark, Chicago

It's hard to remember now how little real barbecue there was on the north side just a few years ago, before these guys got lines out the door every night. Now lots of people are following the dream of making the Texas barbecue they see on the Food Network in Chicago. But Smoque remains the standard, not only because they do BBQ in quantity so well, but because they manage their busy restaurant to keep everybody calm and happy. Anyone thinking of opening a restaurant should watch them in action sometime. *What to order:* brisket, pulled pork, St. Louis ribs, Mikeska sausage.

37. Osteria Langhe

Logan Square • Italian • $$
2824 W. Armitage, Chicago 773-661-1582

There's too little regionality in Italian food in Chicago—or maybe it's dominated by the brusque flavors of one region, Sicily—so a neighborhood restaurant devoted to the Langhe and Piemonte is to be cheered on that basis alone. The food of chef Cameron Grant makes skillful, satisfying use of the region's meats and cheeses (it's as Swiss-leaning as it's stereotypically Italian), not to mention its white Alba truffles in season, while owner Aldo Zaninotto, a wine importer, covers that end with well-chosen recommendations. *What to order:* vitello tonnato, plin, tajarin, coniglio.

38. EL Ideas

Little Village • Fine Dining • $$$$
2419 W. 14th, Chicago 312-226-8144

Phillip Foss wasn't the first person to do a high end pop-up in a low-end space, but as a name chef making the journey to casual food (he had a food truck and this was his prep space) and back again, he kicked off the idea that you could serve fine dining food while guests wandered into the kitchen to take pictures and the chefs chatted with everybody. With others to compare him to now, I don't think Foss has as personal a point of view on food as some like Iliana Regan—he's making likably playful upscale plates, using the things chefs like to use, from foie to wagyu to black cod, schmeared and swirled on the plate. What's most personal here is Foss's conviction that he can make food just fine without a boss and a big hotel around him, and give everybody a good time. His party is your party. *What to order:* tasting menu; BYO wine.

39. Chi Cafe

Chinatown • Chinese, Dim Sum • $
2160 S. Archer Ave., Chicago 312-842-9993

Some reviews of this place refer to it, a little dismissively, as a Chinese diner, especially sitting next to posh and a bit pretentious Ming Hin toward the west end of the Chinatown mall. Hey, I *like* diners, they make tasty food which comes out fast and which nobody can screw up too badly—and anyway, after a remodeling a couple of years ago, the space-age-psychedelia look here is less Diner Grill than Chinese space station. (Beware of the tree stumps that pass for seats at some tables. You think I exaggerate.) *What to order:* I'm not going to claim encyclopedic knowledge of the multi-page menu, but you can't go wrong with anything that starts with "salt and pepper," or anything in XO sauce like the rolled noodles or the turnip cake; the tightly shrimp-packed wontons in the wonton soup are great, and sizzling beef tenderloin is a favorite.

40. Bavette's Bar & Boeuf

Near North Side, River North • Steak • $$$
218 W. Kinzie, Chicago 312-624-8154

Until Green Street Smoked Meats, all of Brendan Sodikoff's restaurants had roughly the same decadent Men's Club For Vampires look. But if ever there was a genre that could use some Anne Rice or something to make it hip, it was the Chicago steakhouse, and not surprisingly, Bavette's has pretty much been booked solid since it opened. *What to order:* steaks are fine but you can find more painstaking tending of your chosen piece of meat elsewhere; better to look at it as a total evening, with oysters, appetizers like the meatball (huge and despite that, one of the best in town), and for a bargain entree that may beat the steaks, the excellent fried chicken.

41. Isla Pilipina

Lincoln Square, Ravenswood • Filipino • $$
2501 W. Lawrence, Chicago 773-271-2988

The first time I went to Isla Pilipina, it was a strip mall hole in the wall with, shall we say, a late night crowd (find a thread at LTHForum called "Transsexual Fried Chicken Taste Off" for more details). A decade later, with the American-raised kids having taken it over, it's a handsome family restaurant that's packed on weekends for highly assured versions of Filipino comfort food. *What to order:* lumpia, arroz caldo (chicken and rice), pancit bihon (noodles), lechon kawali (deep fried pork belly with gravy), bicol express. BYO; there's Filipino and craft beer in the same mall.

42. Big Guys Sausage Stand

Berwyn • Burgers, Hot Dogs • $
7021 Roosevelt Road, Berwyn, 708-317-5213

In a vintage 50s hot dog stand, owner Brendan O'Connor not only cooks up Vienna dogs, but housemade sausages, a terrific handpatted burger, pretty good Italian beef and freshcut fries. In other words, you were looking for another Hot Doug's? It's in Berwyn. *What to order:* Italian sausage, smoked hot link, bacon wrapped cheddar brat, Big Guy Burger.

43. Owen & Engine

Logan Square, Bucktown • Gastropub, Beer, English • $$
2700 N. Western, Chicago 773-235-2930

With its almost EPCOT-esque evocation of an English pub, and a straightforward bar menu, Owen & Engine didn't seem as hip when it opened as new places like Longman & Eagle, but it has aged well; the food is extremely well made and easy to like, the setting is relaxing, and the craft beer list (complete with a few served via an ale engine) is outstanding. *What to order:* burger, fish & chips, half chicken.

44. BRGRBelly

Portage Park • Burgers • $$
5739 W. Irving Park, Chicago 773-283-7880

Jefferson Park • Burgers • $$
5691 N. Milwaukee, Chicago 773-775-6650

Thick "bar burgers" are everywhere and at that price point it's not that hard to do them pretty well, so how does one place make it onto a list like this ahead of the rest? Freshly-ground meat; buns baked in house that leave the plastic-bagged 8-pack type far behind; fun toppings that don't get too wild, like the Midnight Special with frito pie toppings; good freshcut fries; decent craft beer selection; and a relaxed northwest side neighborhood atmosphere, the VH-1 to Kuma's Headbangers Ball. *What to order:* Midnight Special, Old Time Religion, Amazing Grace.

45. Furious Spoon

Wicker Park • Japanese • $$
1571 N. Milwaukee, Chicago 773-687-8445

Logan Square • Japanese • $$
2410 N. Milwaukee, Chicago 773-770-3559

The Loop • Japanese • $$
Revival Food Hall, 125 S. Clark, Chicago 773-999-9411

Before I went to Japan, I wasn't sure if the criterion I was using for ramen—the thick porkiness of the stock—was really what Japan prized. Well, I've been there now, ate ramen a couple of times in Tokyo... and I still don't know. But I remain consistently impressed by the (French as much as Japanese) porky thickness of the stockmaking here, and the springy housemade noodles; I also liked the spritz of lime on the tsukemen, a probably un-Japanese but smart and welcome touch. So right or not, it works for me. *What to order:* ramen (not the spiciest one; doctor it yourself), tsukemen.

46. Dusek's Board & Beer
Pilsen • Gastropub, Beer, Brunch • $$
1227 W. 18th, Chicago 312-526-3851

Dusek's is expert comfort food from the Longman & Eagle team in a retro cocktail bar setting inside a 19th century opera house from Pilsen's days as a Czech neighhborhood. There's also a bar downstairs called Punch House which serves punches and fondue—which always struck me as a silly way to eat, but was surprisingly good with their cuts of housemade charcuterie and the like—and yet another bar in the old horse barn. In short, a satisfyingly modern place from which to watch the gentrification of Pilsen. *What to order:* flat iron steak, Juicy Lucy, suckling pig, broccoli steak.

47. Cemitas Puebla
Near West Side, West Loop • Mexican, Sandwiches • $$
817 W. Fulton Market, Chicago 312-455-9200

Logan Square • Mexican, Sandwiches • $$
3129 W. Armitage, Chicago 773-486-8080

Hyde Park • Mexican, Sandwiches • $$
1321 E. 57th, Chicago 773-420-3631

This is one where Chicago should take a collective bow. An entrepreneur starts making the food of his family's hometown— Mexican sandwiches in the style of Puebla. He does it seriously— he imports the right cheese, gets a bakery to make the right bread

Phillip Foss plating at EL Ideas

and so on, even has his folks grow the herb no one sells here. It attracts a Mexican audience, and an audience of foodies who realize it's something special, and lots of local media, which leads to national media. Eventually it attracts investors, and so there's three of them now, all busy, one of them on the same strip as The Publican and Next. It's a great time to be alive and eating in Chicago. *What to order:* Milanesa, Carne Asada cemitas; tacos al arabe.

48. The Blanchard

Lincoln Park • French • $$$
1935 N. Lincoln Park West, Chicago 872-829-3971

The Blanchard's appearance, in a windowed room at the bottom of a Lincoln Park apartment building, was the answer to the prayers of Chicago's underserved Francophiles, with chef Jason Paskewitz turning out letter-perfect or at most, only modestly modernized takes on French classics (some from the L'Escoffier era, others from the Robuchon or Palladin 80s and 90s). Beware a tendency to oversalt fish dishes, for some reason, if you're sensitive to that. *What to order:* oeuf outhier, escargots à la bourguignonne, any of the foie gras courses, carre d'agneau, duck a l'orange.

49. Pleasant House Pub

Pilsen • English, Beer • $$
2119 S. Halsted, Chicago 773-523-7437

Maybe the most inexplicable Michelin choice of all was never recognizing Pleasant House Bakery as a Bib Gourmand— incredibly satisfying, literally farm to table (they grew some of their greens down the block) English savory pies, very tourist friendly, that would return change from a $10. What could be Bibbier than that? Maybe now that they're in the former Nightwood space, with beer on tap and some other items like fish & chips, the French will appreciate their Englishness. *What to order:* Chicken balti pie, mushroom and kale pie, fish & chips, housemade ginger fizz.

50. Carniceria Aguascalientes
Little Village • Mexican • $
3132 W. 26th, Chicago 773-254-3466

Some of the best handmade tortillas in the city are patted out by
the ladies in the cafeteria of this La Villita grocery store —but note
that you only get them with certain things, so skip the usual carne
asada tacos and order something more substantial like a guisado
(stew) or gooey, soap-like chicharron stewed in a fiery green sauce,
a real mind-expander. *What to order:* pork in mole rojo, chicharron
in mole verde.

51. Momotaro
West Loop, Near West Side • Japanese, Sushi • $$$
820 W. Lake, Chicago 312-733-4818

Like Eataly, Momotaro is less a restaurant than a choice of
restaurants under one handsomely chic roof. The front of the
restaurant is a bar, set up wittily to resemble a trading floor—no
doubt a comforting look for much of the see and be seen crowd
clustering here. Midway through the room is the sushi bar, and
the sushi fish is largely imported through Tsukiji in Japan—you
can sit at the sushi bar, and direct connection with the chefs (or
the omakase) may be a good idea because in my experience,
your desire for the most artful or interesting things can be tough
to communicate through a server. The cooked food, much of it
prepared over the binchotan grills in the kitchen windows, is easier
to get and full of inventive things; it probably gets short shrift with
many sushi-minded customers, as does this more sedate back part
of the room, but don't make their mistake.

Finally, downstairs there's the Izakaya, a dark, much less ritzy
bar—and since besides the izakaya menu you can order anything
from upstairs down here as well, this more intimate space might be
the best place to devote serious attention to the food (though I'm
not wild about the sweet cocktails; do like the Japanese and drink
beer or whisky). *What to order:* chef's sushi or sashimi selection;
amadai no robatayaki, momotaro tartare, chili mentaiko spaghetti;
Izakaya: uni chorizo toast, wagyu beef tongue, pork belly ramen.

52. Manny's Cafeteria and Delicatessen

South Loop • Sandwiches, Deli • $$
1141 S, Jefferson, Chicago 312-939-2855

Manny's isn't the only Jewish deli in the Chicago area—not least because it only recently added a true deli section in addition to its cafeteria line—but it's indisputably one-of-a-kind, a bustling 1950s-era crossroads of the city where pols, city workers and tourists come together for the love of corned beef, and to get gently ribbed by Gino, who mans the slicer. The new deli part, at the other end of the building from the traditional cafeteria line, finally adds smoked fish and other lighter items, which join the cafeteria offerings on the line. *What to order:* Corned beef (not lean, if you want proper flavor and texture), pastrami, reuben, short ribs, knishes.

53. Animale

Bucktown, Logan Square • Italian, Sandwiches, Breakfast • $$
1904 N. Western, Chicago 872-315-3912

From the owner and chef of Osteria Langhe, a quick service sandwich and pasta place focused on offal meats, bringing hardcore Italian peasant funkiness to Bucktown/Logan Square. Beyond that there are some good pastas, all small plates style, as well as a pretty tasty burger (made with domestic Piedmontese beef, of course), and a few well-curated wine choices that change frequently. When food like this is in the $10, we'll-call-your-number range, you know we've achieved civilization at last. *What to order:* lingua & coda, cuore e cuore, tartufo nero, arancini.

54. Cellar Door Provisions

Avondale, Logan Square • Bakery, Farm To Table • $$
3025 W. Diversey, Chicago 773-697-8337

Admirers love its beautifully made, very natural farm to table food and exceptional baked goods; scoffers scoff at the prices for a single slice of bread topped with some beets and cheese, and the fact that its baking schedule follows a slacking hipster's idea of when things should be ready for breakfast. I can see both points of view, but the mahogany-colored croissants are about the best in town and the dark, crusty bread is as bitter as coffee grounds, and wonderful. *What to order:* croissants, tartine, quiche.

55. The Budlong
The Loop · Chicken · $$
Revival Food Hall, 125 S. Clark, Chicago 773-270-9005

Nashville hot chicken has become a thing here but there's probably more of it that's not very good than is, heat carelessly applied to make it a challenge to eat. It took Jared Leonard, of Rub Country Smokehouse on the north side, to crack the code on both fried chicken and the right heat for a burn that warms from the inside without torching. The Budlong's travails since then have been widely reported, at the moment only the Revival Food Hall location is open, but the long-awaited primary location in Lincoln Square (4619 N. Western) and another at 1008 W. Armitage should arrive eventually. *What to order:* Nashville hot chicken, biscuits.

56. Lula Cafe
Logan Square · American, Farm to Table, Breakfast · $$
2537 N. Kedzie, Chicago 773-489-9554

Pioneering restaurant in both Logan Square and in doing farm to table cooking (when that didn't even exist as a term for it), Jason Hammel's Lula Cafe still has its hippie cafe charms—it's a little cramped in a creaky old building, and the art on the wall is guaranteed to be a bit weird. But the quality of the cooking has risen steadily over the years, and current chef Sarah Rinkavage does a skillful job with Lula's menu of mostly comfortable entrees like roast chicken and pastas, while showing more creativity in the appetizers (a fall standout was whole slices of butternut squash, roasted and served with n'duja and gouda). *What to order:* changes seasonally; vegetarian tasting menu, Monday night farm dinner.

57. Ceres' Table
Lakeview · Italian, Pizza · $$
3124 N. Broadway, Chicago 773-922-4020

Ceres' Table founding chef Giuseppe Scurato was Sicilian, but it

always had a more delicate hand than the usual Chicago Italian-Sicilian restaurant blasting out big plates of acidic pasta and tomato sauce. Reinvigorated by new owners who moved it to Lakeview from its previous opposite-the-cemetery location and now under chef Steven O'Neill, its highly accessible food and comfortable room seems to fit right in to a busy strip, with well-crafted housemade pasta dishes and pretty decent pizzas from a woodburning oven. *What to order:* swordfish carpaccio, grilled radicchio, burrata, orrechiette with lamb sausage, spaghetti carbonara, whole grilled branzino; finnochiona pizze bianche.

58. Chiya Chai

Logan Square • Indian, Nepalese, Tea • $$
2770 N. Milwaukee, Chicago 773-360-7541

A family of Nepalese tea importers opened this sunny cafe which serves chai drinks and initially served a small menu of Nepalese-flavored curries, dumplings and savory pies. (They've since opened The Backroom, with a fuller menu.) The chais are excellent and as places to hang with your laptop go, this is a calming, pleasant space. The dumplings, alas, need more work to get the hang of doing the wrappers, but the savory pies are excellent, with flaky crusts and brightly spiced fillings. *What to order:* ginger cardamom chai, chicken balti pie, curried kale and potato pie.

59. J.P. Graziano Grocery Co.

West Loop • Sandwiches, Deli • $
901 W. Randolph, Chicago 312-666-4587

When Marché first launched the West Loop toward being Chicago's hottest dining district in 1993, this Italian grocer and distributor had already been there for 56 years. Today it's mostly out of the wholesale business—though a thick wedge of parmiggiano reggiano is still a standard purchase for me—but its fantastic Italian subs (on crusty coal-fired bread from Damato's nearby) are living history on this fast-changing strip, and there's no hot chef in the neighborhood who doesn't bring them in regularly

Jared Leonard making Nashville Hot chicken for The Budlong

for lunch. *What to order:* Mr. G, prosciutto, porchetta, Will Special (off menu).

60. Boeufhaus
West Town • Steak • $$$
1012 N. Western, Chicago 773-661-2116

As steakhouses grew over more grandiose downtown, this place opened to bring them back to down to earth in the city's neighborhoods, serving a brasserie-style menu as well as selling beef in its meat market up front. The steaks are very good, but the thing that wowed me the most with the care it showed was a crudité plate—between the housemade Green Goddess dressing and the gorgeous, handpicked vegetables, this was a plate that would have warmed James Beard's heart as an example of unfussy, clean-flavored midcentury American food. *What to order:* crudité, shortrib beignets. tartare of boeuf, 55-day aged ribeye; at lunch, reuben, boeuf on weck.

61. Al-Sufara Grills
Palos Hills • Middle Eastern • $$
7215 W, 103rd St., Palos Hills 708-576-8420

For the best middle eastern food in Chicago. go south of Chicago to places like Bridgeview, Worth, Palos Hills; besides a number of authentic restaurants and bakeries, you'll also find a preference for grilling meat over live charcoal at a number of spots (Al-Bawadi, Jerusalem Restaurant, etc.). How do you know they're doing that? Well, in this case the entire parking lot is filled with smoke, and once you go inside this meat market-restaurant, you'll see big cones of lamb and chicken being twirled over glowing coals. Since this is first a meat market, the service is kind of perfunctory, but your tender, smoky reward will not be long in coming. *What to order:* lamb shawerma, kofte kebab, shish tawook, hummus, muttabal.

62. Orsi's Pizza (Chester's)
Summit Argo • Pizza, Italian • $
6255 S. Archer, Summit Argo 708-458-1117

We all know that Vito & Nick's is the best south side thin crust pizza, right? What if there was another place with at least as much history and a thin crust that may beat that famous one? Would it blow your mind? Head to Summit, a hardknuckle suburb on the southwest edge of Chicago, and find Chester's Tavern, which Orsi's sits inside, and prepare to question everything you know—or at least have an afternoon shooting the breeze and drinking beer with the locals. *What to order:* cheese or sausage pizza, but they offer nice homemade Italian specials, too.

63. Go 4 Food

Chinatown • Chinese, Seafood • $$
212 W. 23rd, Chicago 312-842-8688

On the plus side, the Cantonese classics Go 4 Food does well it does really well—for instance, hot and sour soup is a hoary old cliché, but theirs is bright with fresh pepper and vinegar. And it's a real deal for something like red chili Dungeness crab at a decent price, when it's in season. On the minus side, it's always busy and it's in a small multi-level building (as it might well be in a Chinese city), and you may get stuck half-forgotten in the basement. Accept that that's the price of dining in this authentic experience, and good luck with your ordering. *What to order:* Fresh seafood, like steamed razor clams; hot and sour soup; Chinese style ribs; beef chow fun noodles; millionaire fried rice.

64. En Hakkore

Bucktown • Korean • $$
1840 N. Damen, Chicago 773-772-9880

Some people like the paratha tacos, but for me En Hakkore is one dish: their version of bibimbap mixes a little meat and some rice into a beautiful bowl of colorful, crunchy fresh vegetables. It's far from the funkiest bibimbap in town—I wish it had a fresh cooked egg rather than hardboiled slices—but it's very pretty and healthy-tasting. *What to order:* bibimbap, paratha tacos.

65. Forbidden Root

West Town • Beer, American • $$
1746 W. Chicago, Chicago 312-929-2202

The restaurant and bar in an old theater building is kind of vast and charmless, which is too bad, because to me this is the most successful so far of several new places aiming to combine a brewery doing unusual flavorings (mostly spices and botanicals in the beers) with a quality menu of artisanal, global bar food. *What to order:* beer flight, cranberry bean hummus, NBLT, milk-brined pork schnitzel sandwich.

66. Americano 2211

Wicker Park • Cafe, Bakery • $$
2211 W. North, Chicago 773-360-8757

Small cafe with a small menu which has some good simple sandwiches and savory pastries, excellent coffee drinks, a few Mediterranean dishes, and some wonderful cookies and ice cream by Nancy Silver, a veteran of Charlie Trotter's and Blackbird. *What to order:* ham and cheese croquettes, shakshuka, seared halloumi, Sicilian almond cookies.

67. Yusho

Avondale • Japanese, Gastropub • $$
2853 N. Kedzie, Chicago 773-904-8558

Hyde Park • Japanese, Gastropub • $$
1301 E. 53rd, Chicago 773-643-1652

Japanese gastropub—is that a thing? I guess it is now, and has been ever since Matthias Merges, former chef de cuisine at Charlie Trotter's, made this his first solo venture, helping kick off the upscale-downscale Asian thing here. The relaxed atmosphere goes well with the simple but well-crafted Japanese bar snack food and the whiskey-focused bar. *What to order:* fried chicken, chicken dumpling ramen, charred octopus.

68. Aroy Thai

Lincoln Square • Thai • $
4654 N. Damen, Chicago 773-275-8360

Tiny Ravenswood Thai restaurant with a translated "secret" menu pointing to some of the more authentic dishes on the menu; the beef ball and tendon soup, eye-openingly spicy and pungent with tamarind and galangal, is one of my standard orders when I have a cold and I need a miracle cure. *What to order:* pad see eiw, basil pork with century egg, crispy salty fish fried rice, tod mun (fried fish cakes), beef ball and tendon soup.

69. The Duck Inn

Bridgeport • American, Cocktails • $$$
2701 S. Eleanor, Chicago 312-724-8811

Chef Kevin Hickey worked the globe for hotels (winning a Michelin star at The Four Seasons here) before settling back not only in his neighborhood, but in a bar a few doors down from the house he grew up in. The front has a retro-hipster bar, while the backroom and patio are home to his hearty, easy to like calories-be-damned food. *What to order:* rotisserie duck, duck fat dog, hamburger sandwich, crispy chicken thigh.

70. Nomad Pizza Company

Lincoln Square • Pizza • $
4019 N. Damen, Chicago 847-393-3955

Ignore the prep kitchen location, Nomad Pizza is a mobile operation—not exactly a food truck since they haul a big stone woodburning oven—but they're not too hard to track down, since they're usually at the Green City Market in Lincoln Park, as well as various events around town. Anyway, what makes them worth the effort is not only the great Neapolitan pizza with a crust of black-charred bubbles, but the novel combinations they put on them, often using things like peaches from the market. *What to order:* black and white pizza, whatever looks good.

71. Arami

West Town, Ukrainian Village • Sushi, Japanese • $$$
1829 W. Chicago, Chicago 312-243-1535

Arami started as a sushi bar with a few cooked things, and then the sushi chef left (to start Juno), and so they put in some binchotan grills—maybe the first in the city then, or close—and stressed the grilled foods as well. Which has made Arami more interesting ever since—I would put Arami at the high end of mid-priced for sushi, but it's the range of cooked food that makes it a total experience. *What to order:* sushi, maitake (grilled), buta hara.

72. 90 Miles Cuban Café

Roscoe Village • Cuban, Sandwiches • $
3101 N. Clybourn, Chicago 773-248-2822

Logan Square • Cuban, Sandwiches • $
2540 W. Armitage, Chicago 773-227-2822

Not that there's a lot of difference between Cuban sandwiches in Chicago, especially the more authentically made they are, but besides having the best ramshackle-beach-shack atmosphere, these places stand out for some of the other items served alongside your Cubano, from pretty good empanadas to excellent seafood soups. *What to order:* Cubano, Media Noche, Timbra, soup.

73. Stock

West Town • American, Farm to Table, Breakfast • $
1427 W. Willow, Chicago 312-432-6575

The cafe inside the Local Foods grocery is a good place to gauge what's in season (and on sale right next to it), but it's also an easy place to grab a hearty, well crafted meal of fresh ingredients—Chef Abra Berens has been both a farmer supplying local restaurants, and worked at restaurants such as Vie and Floriole Cafe. *What to order:* kale pasty, chicken and dumplings, grilled cheese and tomato soup.

74. D'Candela Restaurant

Irving Park · South American · $$
4053 N. Kedzie, Chicago 773-478-0819

There's an extensive menu here with some good beef and seafood items here, but at least the first time, you're here for one thing: the outstanding Peruvian rotisserie chicken, cooked over blazing coals and served with spicy green aji (sauce). *What to order:* pollo a la brasas, chuoe de camarones, ceviche, empanadas.

75. Rainbow Cuisine

Lincoln Square · Thai · $
4825 N. Western, Chicago 773-754-7660

The owners of this sunny Thai spot (more Ikea than Asian trunk show like most of the Thai places in Lincoln Square) were previously the cooks at Spoon, and patrons of one of the city's first translated Thai "secret menus" will recognize many of the dishes, good as ever. *What to order:* gai tawt (Thai fried chicken), nam khao tawt, boat noodles, isaan sausage, som tum (papaya salad).

76. Cai

Chinatown · Chinese, Dim Sum · $$
2100 S. Archer Ave. 2F, Chicago 312-326-6888

Slightly fancy (in a banquet hall way), Cai serves dinner, but I've only been there for one thing: dim sum. The dim sum is good, but it's also very accessible because the room is busy with servers pushing carts, and the paper menu has pictures of everything. On that basis, there's no place that better fits my mental picture of how a dim sum place should be. (And I'm not the only one; on weekends, go early or be prepared to wait, behind lots of Chinese families.) *What to order:* barbecued pork bun, shrimp har gow, shu mai, xiao long bao, Portuguese egg tarts.

77. Nhu Lan Bakery

Lincoln Square, Ravenswood • Vietnamese, Sandwiches • $
2612 W. Lawrence, Chicago 773-878-9898

Uptown • Vietnamese, Sandwiches • $
4810 N. Sheridan, Chicago 773-944-9288

Vietnamese banh mi sandwiches have started popping up around town, but there's rarely a real comparison to this pioneering Vietnamese-owned shop (which finally has been convinced to adopt American attitudes toward refrigeration). Most of the sandwiches come with a schmear of livery paté, crisp vegetables and some jalapeño, and they all combine hot and fresh and funky in a way that screams tropical flavors. There are assorted other things to be had, from pho to bubble teas to bbq pork buns, to complete your experience. *What to order:* original, lemongrass pork, vegan lemongrass tofu.

78. Smalls. Smoke Shack & More

Irving Park • Barbecue • $
4009 N. Albany, Chicago 312-857-4221

For a while my measurement for fine dining was, "Would I rather have just gotten some barbecue from Smalls?" Texas-style barbecue crossed with Asian flavors, they make terrific brisket and pulled pork with Asian dipping sauces and what they call "not slaw," but the fusion really blasts into orbit with the BBQ brisket bibimbop, which you can get with either white or Filipino garlic rice, depending on how much of the funk you can handle. *What to order:* brisket, bbq brisket bibimbop, fried chicken, garlic rice.

79. Canton Regio

Pilsen • Mexican • $$
1510 W. 18th, Chicago 312-733-3045

The tragedy of the burning of venerable Pilsen spot Nuevo Leon is at least somewhat mitigated by this new place from the same family,

Left: Paco's Tacos

which aims to recreate the experience of grilled meat halls in Mexican cities like Oaxaca, where skirt steak is bought by the kilo (about 2 lbs.) and grilled to order. It doesn't quite capture the total sensory overload of that experience (probably a good thing), but it smells as good, and the kilo of meat with freshly-griddled corn and flour tortillas is primally satisfying (and will feed 3-4). *What to order:* a kilo; sweetbreads.

80. Pub Royale

West Town, Ukrainian Village • Indian, English, Beer • $$
2049 W. Division, Chicago 773-661-6874

I haven't been to England in long enough that I have no idea if British-Indian fusion pubs like this really exist. But they'll seem like they should after enjoying the well-chosen midwestern craft beer list alongside bright, piquant curries and paratha here, with the occasional Britishism like a pot pie thrown in. (There's also a burger, which bears the only possible name—Royale with cheese.) *What to order:* lamb dumplings, butter chicken, chicken tikka kathi roll.

81. Bang Bang Pie & Biscuits

Logan Square • Breakfast, Bakery • $
2051 N. California, Chicago 773-276-8888

Lincoln Square, Ravenswood • Breakfast, Bakery • $
4947 N. Damen, Chicago 773-530-9020

Pie is good at this pie shop, and pie for breakfast is something there's just not enough of in Chicago, but the surprise here is not just that the biscuits are good (everyone knows that) but how sophisticated the biscuit have gotten as balanced dishes, even if something like the brisket biscuit will sock you out till early afternoon. *What to order:* Bacon biscuit, gravy biscuit, farmer's biscuit; classic apple pie.

82. Cafe Marie-Jeanne

Humboldt Park • French, Breakfast • $$
1001 N. California, Chicago 773-904-7660

Michael Simmons, long of Rootstock across the street, launched this French-tinged café (in the French, we-serve-wine sense) which makes some of everything for every part of the day, most of it earthy, warm and comfy. In Montreal Marie-Jeanne is your old aunt, and this place is as welcoming as one. *What to order:* housemade croissants, maple pecan oatmeal; lobster bisque; smoked chicken, smoked and pickled fishes.

83. Spinning J Bakery and Soda Fountain
Humboldt Park · American, Breakfast · $$
1000 N. California, Chicago 872-829-2793

...and across the street from Cafe Marie-Jeanne's French cafe is a pure American one, sweetly evoking 1920s soda fountains and lunch counters, with light sandwiches and soups and excellent pie—and real phosphates. If you have to ask what that is, just go have one right now. *What to order:* sandwiches, quiche, key lime hibiscus pie, strawberry-watermelon phosphate.

84. Saigon Bistro
West Rogers Park · Vietnamese, Seafood · $$
6244 N. California, Chicago 773-564-9336

Located in the same far north strip mall as Gogi, this Vietnamese restaurant (which at first glance could be an Irish bar) is a cut above for several Asian standbys, including hot pot, pho, and especially the sudden Chicago craze for Vietnamese-Cajun crawfish in spicy seasonings. Which here, has the dimensionality of flavor that's lacking at those better known places for angry critters. *What to order:* Crawgish Cajun Fusion, pho Saigon, hot pot, banh xeo, goi du du (Vietnamese papaya salad).

85. Xi'an Cuisine
Chinatown · Chinese, Sandwiches · $
225 W. Cermak, Chicago 312-326-3171

From partly Muslim northwest China come these little pita-like sandwiches filled with spicy lamb and other fillings; they also serve hand-stretched noodle dishes, tasty and dirt cheap. *What to order:*

lamb with cumin, pork or marinated beef in flatbread sandwiches; hand-stretched noodles in hot oil and soy sauce.

86. Ivy's Burgers, Hot Dogs and Fries

Edgebrook • Burgers, Hot Dogs • $
5419 W. Devon, Chicago 773-775-2545

Edgebrook has a 1950s suburb feel, and so it has to have a dog and burger stand for the whole family, right? Ivy's takes that model and updates it just enough for the 2010s, with reclaimed wood tables and some modern spins. The dogs (Eisenberg) include some international novelties like a Japanese dog (seaweed and ginger) or Danish dog (brown mustard and crispy onions); the burgers are dead ringers for the big, juicy ones at Des Plaines' Paradise Pup; the freshcut fries come with use of a bar of different salts, the shakes use Homer's ice cream; and the friendliness makes you feel like you belong to the neighborhood. *What to order:* Japan dog, burger with Merkt's cheddar, green chile burger.

87. Paco's Tacos (Supermercado La Internacional)

Back of the Yards • Mexican • $
4556 S. Ashland, Chicago

I could fill this book with candidates for best steak tacos, which is why I long kept Zacatacos on south Pulaski as my standard don't-have-to-think-about-it answer—but I hear reports of decline there and haven't had the heart to follow them up. So I elevate another candidate, located inside a grocery, to official #1 status. Note that there are other Paco's Tacos around the south side, but the Pulaski one, at least, does not measure up (especially being across the street from the original Zacatacos). *What to order:* tacos with carne asada (steak), carnitas, barbacoa.

88. Johnny's Grill

Logan Square • Diner, Irish, Breakfast • $$
2545 N. Kedzie, Chicago 773-278-2215

A real diner becomes a faux hipster diner—sign of everything wrong with America, right? Well, but chef Sarah Jordan is Irish, and it's pretty tough to argue with her Irish breakfast and lunch as not being a net plus for the neighborhood—and true to the spirit of what this corner grill used to be. *What to order:* double cheeseburger, Irish breakfast, breakfast pie, Irish bacon BAP.

89. Burritos Juarez

West Lawn • Mexican • $
5935 S. Pulaski, Chicago 773-306-2314

Chicago Mexican is about tacos; the typical overstuffed burrito is for drunken bros late at night. But the exception to that rule is this place, whose norteño-style burritos are not overstuffed, but expertly crafted; order 2 or 3. For more, see Hunter Owens' "The Fooditor Guide to the Norteño Burritos at Burritos Juarez." *What to order:* deshebrada burrito, barbacoa burrito, rajas con queso burrito, chile relleno burrito.

90. Brown Sugar Bakery

Greater Grand Crossing • Bakery • $
328 E. 75th, Chicago 773-224-6262

You may have had this place's caramel cupcakes at Lem's or Macarthur's, among others. They're fantastic, and so is pretty much everything else in this bakery, and everybody is nice as could be. *What to order:* caramel cake, sweet potato pie, Obama cake ("Sort of like America, it's chocolate cake, yellow cake, red velvet cake, white frosting, covered with chocolate frosting—and nuts").

91. Ramen Misoya

Mount Prospect • Japanese • $
1584 S. Busse Rd., Mount Prospect, 847-437-4590

Near North Side • Japanese • $
213 E. Ohio, Chicago 815-770-5857

A Japanese chain with two Chicago-area locations, serving impeccably made ramen in various styles associated with different cities. The Mount Prospect one has an evocative Tokyo diner feel worth the trip from the city for the complete package; there's also a downtown location, which seems to rank a little lower but still among the better ramen in the city. *What to order:* kome miso, Hokkaido style, for a porkier ramen; shiro miso, Kyoto style, for a lighter style; chashu (pork cheek slices) add-on in any case.

92. Interurban Cafe and Pastry Shop
Lincoln Park • Bakery • $
2008 N. Halsted [enter off Armitage], Chicago 773-698-7739

The first thing I love about this place is that it's hidden in an alley and just *sort of* looks like a lunch spot and bakery inside. Honestly, what it looks like is that the next time you come here, it'll turn out you dreamed it. But the soups, sandwiches and pastries (from a former Charlie Trotter's pastry chef) are just fine. *What to order:* spinach, red pepper and goat cheese tartlet; pop tarts, morning buns.

93. Cafe Orchid
Lakeview, Roscoe Village • Turkish • $$
1746 W. Addison, Chicago 773-327-3808

Modest, family-run Turkish cafe gives a convincing feel of an Istanbul restaurant (all it's lacking is hard-drinking Australians; it's BYO, incidentally). *What to order:* Iskender kebab, imim bayildi, kabobs, baba ghanoush.

94. Annapurna
West Rogers Park • Indian/Pakistani, Vegetarian • $
2608 W. Devon, Chicago 773-764-1858

A longtime Devon place known for hole-in-the-wall atmosphere and tasty, no-frills vegetarian food, Annapurna got spiffed up (and a friendlier generation seems to have taken over) several years ago but its other virtues remain the same. *What to order:* Chole bhatura, Gujarati khali, raj kachori chaat ("Indian tacos"), dosa.

95. The Kitchen Bistro

River North • Italian, Farm to Table • $$$
316 N. Clark, Chicago 312-836-1300

Is there a better chef hiding in plain sight than Johnny Anderes, of the late and beloved Telegraph, working at the River North outpost of a Colorado-based chain? It has a star location (on the river) but no one seems to be paying it any attention because it is yet another chain, with a name that redefines "generic," serving Italian and American food in that area. Yet the pastas I tried—like a squid ink spaghetti with lemon and bitter toasted bread crumbs— were about as good as any in the city, the corporate commitment to farm to table seems for real, and, well, they didn't go cheap on the view. *What to order:* seasonal pastas and meats.

96. Magic Jug

Dunning • Ukrainian • $$
6354 W. Irving Park, Chicago 773-286-8855

There's not much Ukrainian food left in Chicago, and even less that's good, but this welcoming place on the northwest side will make you feel at home on a cold winter day with varenyky (pierogi), borsch and other ribsticking dishes. *What to order:* chanakhy soup, borsch, cheburek (meat pie), varenyky, galushky (potato dumplings with gravy).

97. Kimski

Bridgeport • Korean, Polish • $$
960 W. 31st, Chicago 773-890-0588

The family behind Bridgeport's beloved Maria's bar is Polish-Korean, so that inspired adding on this restaurant with a short but tasty list of meaty drinking foods inspired by a shared love for pork and fermented cabbage. *What to order:* Maria's standard (Korean-polish sausage), scallion potato pancakes, Kimski poutine.

98. Hetman Deli

Cragin • Polish, Deli • $
5513 W. Belmont, Chicago 773-282-1583

I've tried lots of Polish restaurants over the years, though one of the first, Smak Tak on north Elston, remains the favorite—for a restaurant. (My old Chowhound post was probably the first thing anybody wrote about it... and now it's a Michelin Bib Gourmand. *I'm just sayin'...*) But it wasn't until I did a piece on Eastern European food in Chicago for Thrillist that I really grasped the truth about this food, which is... it's not about restaurants. Instead, look in the Polish groceries, delis and bakeries, like this one on west Belmont, for the widest variety of ribsticking hearty food for the long Chicago winters. *What to order:* smoked whole pig, anything in the case that looks good (very little English, so point).

99. Mortar & Pestle

Lakeview • Breakfast • $$
3108 N. Broadway, Chicago 773-857-2087

Here's an idea: brunch for breakfast. Mortar & Pestle serves well-crafted, global-trendy breakfast and lunch food with a full bar, making it more like a Sunday brunch spot than a diner; the food's on the rich side but not as gut-punchy as, say, Au Cheval. The prices match the ambition, but, you know, that's real crab meat on the benedict, that sort of thing. *What to order:* merguez biscuits and gravy, benedict with crab and sriracha hollandaise, avocado toast.

RESTAURANTS BY TYPE

AMERICAN
5. Boka
11. Vie
17. The Bristol
25. The Publican
56. Lula Cafe
65. Forbidden Root
69. The Duck Inn
73. Stock
83. Spinning J Bakery and Soda Fountain

BAKERY
24. Hoosier Mama Pie Co.
54. Cellar Door Provisions
81. Bang Bang Pie & Biscuits
83. Spinning J Bakery and Soda Fountain
90. Brown Sugar Bakery
92. Interurban Cafe and Pastry Shop

BARBECUE
19. Honey 1 BBQ
36. Smoque
78. Smalls, Smoke Smack & More

BEER
25. The Publican
43. Owen & Engine
46. Dusek's Board & Beer
49. Pleasant House Pub
65. Forbidden Root
80. Pub Royale

BREAKFAST
6. Snaggletooth
12. Arbor
29. Publican Quality Meats
53. Animale
56. Lula Cafe
73. Stock
81. Bang Bang Pie & Biscuits
82. Cafe Marie-Jeanne
88. Johnny's Grill
99. Mortar & Pestle

BRUNCH
1. Fat Rice
25. The Publican
46. Dusek's Board & Beer

BURGERS
33. Red Hot Ranch
42. Big Guys Sausage Stand
44. BRGRBelly
86. Ivy's Burgers, Hot Dogs & Fries

CHICKEN
28. 5 Loaves Eatery
55. The Budlong
74. D'Candela

CHINESE
1. Fat Rice
39. Chi Cafe
63. Go 4 Food
76. Cai
85. Xi'an Cuisine

COCKTAILS
16. The Milk Room
69. The Duck Inn

CONTEMPORARY
3. Giant
5. Boka
10. Blackbird

CUBAN
72. 90 Miles Cuban Café

DELI
6. Snaggletooth
29. Publican Quality Meats
52. Manny's Cafeteria and Delicatessen
59. J.P. Graziano Grocery Co.
98. Hetman Deli

DIM SUM
39. Chi Cafe
76. Cai

DINER
88. Johnny's Grill

ENGLISH/IRISH
43. Owen & Engine
49. Pleasant House Pub
80. Pub Royale
88. Johnny's Grill

EUROPEAN
34. Table, Donkey & Stick

FARM TO TABLE
7. Smyth & The Loyalist
10. Blackbird
11. Vie
12. Arbor
17. The Bristol
54. Cellar Door Provisions
56. Lula Cafe
73. Stock
95. The Kitchen Bistro

FILIPINO
41. Isla Pilipina

FINE DINING
4. Oriole
7. Smyth & The Loyalist
14. 42 Grams
32. Elizabeth
38. EL Ideas

FRENCH
48. The Blanchard
82. Cafe Marie-Jeanne

GASTROPUB
43 Owen & Engine
46. Dusek's Board & Beer
67. Yusho

GRILL
20. Khan BBQ
21. El Che Bar

HOT DOGS
33. Red Hot Ranch
42. Big Guys Sausage Stand

INDIAN/PAKISTANI
20. Khan BBQ
58. Chiya Cafe
80. Pub Royale
94. Annapurna

ITALIAN
13. The Purple Pig
23. Monteverde
37. Osteria Langhe
53. Animale
57. Ceres' Table
62. Orsi's Pizza (Chester's)
95. The Kitchen Bistro

JAPANESE
22. Sumi Robata Bar
45. Furious Spoon
51. Momotaro
67. Yusho
71. Arami
91. Ramen Misoya

KOREAN
8. Hanbun
64. En Hakkore
97. Kimski

MEXICAN
2. Birrieria Zaragoza
26. La Chapparita
31. Leña Brava
47. Cemitas Puebla
50. Carniceria Aguascalientes
79. Canton Regio
87. Paco's Tacos
89. Burritos Juarez

MIDDLE EASTERN
61. Al-Sufara Grills

NEPALESE
58. Chiya Cafe

PIZZA
15. Coalfire
57. Ceres' Table
62. Orsi's Pizza (Chester's)
70. Nomad Pizza Company

POLISH
97. Kimski
98. Hetman Deli

SANDWICHES
29. Publican Quality Meats
47. Cemitas Puebla
52. Manny's Cafeteria and Delicatessen
53. Animale
59. J.P. Graziano Grocery Co.
72. 90 Miles Cuban Café
77. Nhu Lan Bakery
85. Xi'an Cuisine

SEAFOOD
6. Snaggletooth
18. mfk
31. Leña Brava
63. Go 4 Food
84. Saigon Bistro

SMALL PLATES
3. Giant
9. Vera
13. The Purple Pig

SOUTH AMERICAN
21. El Che Bar
74. D'Candela

SOUL FOOD
28. 5 Loaves Eatery

SPANISH
9. Vera
18. mfk

STEAK
40. Bavette's Bar & Boeuf
60. Boeufhaus

SUSHI
51. Momotaro
71. Arami

TASTING MENU
4. Oriole
7. Smyth & The Loyalist
8. Hanbun
10. Blackbird
12. Arbor
14. 42 Grams
32. Elizabeth
38. EL Ideas

TEA
58. Chiya Cafe

THAI
30. Immm Rice and Beyond
68. Aroy Thai
75. Rainbow Cuisine

TURKISH
93. Cafe Orchid

UKRAINIAN
96, Magic Jug

VEGETARIAN
94. Annapurna

VIETNAMESE
35. Nha Hang Viet Nam
77. Nhu Lan Bakery
84. Saigon Bistro

WINE BAR
9. Vera
34. Table, Donkey & Stick

RESTAURANTS BY LOCATION

NORTH SIDE

AVONDALE
27. Parachute
54. Cellar Door Provisions
67. Yusho

BUCKTOWN
17. The Bristol
43. Owen & Engine
53. Animale
64. En Hakkore

CHINATOWN
39. Chi Cafe
63. Go 4 Food
76. Cai
85. Xi'an Cuisine

CRAGIN
98. Hetman Deli

DUNNING
96. Magic Jug

EDGEBROOK
86. Ivy's Burgers, Hot Dogs and Fries

HUMBOLDT PARK
82. Cafe Marie-Jeanne
83. Spinning J Bakery & Soda Fountain

IRVING PARK
36. Smoque
74. D'Candela Restaurant
78. Smalls. Smoke Shack & More

JEFFERSON PARK
44. BRGRBelly

LAKEVIEW
6. Snaggletooth
15. Coalfire
18. mfk
33. Red Hot Ranch
57. Ceres' Table
93. Cafe Orchid
99. Mortar & Pestle

LINCOLN PARK
5. Boka
48. The Blanchard
92. Interurban Cafe and Pastry Shop

LINCOLN SQUARE
32. Elizabeth
41. Isla Pilipina
68. Aroy Thai
75. Rainbow Cuisine
77. Nhu Lan Bakery
81. Bang Bang Pie & Biscuits

LOGAN SQUARE
1. Fat Rice
3. Giant
12. Arbor
34. Table, Donkey & Stick
37. Osteria Langhe
43. Owen & Engine
45. Furious Spoon
47. Cemitas Puebla
53. Animale
54. Cellar Door Provisions
56. Lula Cafe
58. Chiya Chai
72. 90 Miles Cuban Café
81. Bang Bang Pie & Biscuits
88. Johnny's Grill

LOOP, THE
16. The Milk Room
45. Furious Spoon
47. Cemitas Puebla
55. The Budlong

NEAR NORTH SIDE
13. The Purple Pig
40. Bavette's Bar and Boeuf
91. Ramen Misoya

NEAR WEST SIDE
4. Oriole
9. Vera
10. Blackbird
31. Leña Brava
47. Cemitas Puebla
51. Momotaro

PORTAGE PARK
44. BRGRBelly

RIVER NORTH
22. Sumi Robata Bar
40. Bavette's Bar and Boeuf
95. The Kitchen Bistro

ROSCOE VILLAGE
72. 90 Miles Cuban Café
93. Cafe Orchid

UKRAINIAN VILLAGE
24. Hoosier Mama Pie Co.
71. Arami
80. Pub Royale

UPTOWN
14. 42 Grams
30. Immm Rice and Beyond
35. Nha Hang Viet Nam
77. Nhu Lan Bakery

WEST LOOP
4. Oriole
7. Smyth & The Loyalist
9. Vera
10. Blackbird
21. El Che Bar
23. Monteverde
25. The Publican
29. Publican Quality Meats
31. Leña Brava
47. Cemitas Puebla
51. Momotaro
59. J.P. Graziano Grocery Co.

WEST ROGERS PARK
20. Khan BBQ
84. Saigon Bistro
94. Annapurna

WEST TOWN
15. Coalfire
24. Hoosier Mama Pie Co.

60. Boeufhaus
66. Forbidden Root
71. Arami
73. Stock
80. Pub Royale

WICKER PARK
45. Furious Spoon
66. Americano 2211

SOUTH SIDE

ARCHER HEIGHTS
2. Birrieria Zaragoza

BACK OF THE YARDS
87. Paco's Tacos (Supermer-cado La Internacional)

BRIDGEPORT
69. The Duck Inn
97. Kimski

GRAND BOULEVARD
19. Honey 1 BBQ

GREATER GRAND CROSSING
28. 5 Loaves Eatery
90. Brown Sugar Bakery

HYDE PARK
47. Cemitas Puebla
67. Yusho

LITTLE VILLAGE
26. La Chaparrita

38. EL Ideas
50. Carniceria Aguascalientes

PILSEN
46. Dusek's Board & Beer
49. Pleasant House Pub
79. Canton Regio

SOUTH LOOP
52. Manny's Cafeteria and Delicatessen

WEST LAWN
89. Burritos Juarez

SUBURBS

BERWYN
42. Big Guys Sausage Stand

EVANSTON
24. Hoosier Mama Pie Co.

MOUNT PROSPECT
91. Ramen Misoya

PALOS HILLS
61. Al-Sufara Grills

SUMMIT ARGO
62. Orsi's Pizza (Chester's)

WESTERN SPRINGS
11. Vie

WESTMONT
8. Hanbun

ABOUT THE AUTHOR

Michael Gebert is the publisher and editor of Fooditor, recognized as the go-to source for in-depth and thoughtful longform coverage of the Chicago dining scene, from high end to hot dog joints.

He worked at top ad agencies in Chicago for many years, and while working freelance after the dot-com crash and other c. 2000 disasters, started wasting time chatting about Chicago food on Chowhound.com. He was one of the participants there who went on to found LTHForum, a Chicago-based food chat site which democratized talking and writing about food in Chicago during the mid-2000s.

He began writing for Chicago publications including the Chicago *Reader* and *Time Out Chicago*, and has written for national publications such as Saveur.com, *Maxim*, Air Canada's magazine and First We Feast. He was the editor of *New York* magazine's Grub Street Chicago for two years, and subsequently a thrice-weekly columnist for the Reader. He enjoyed national attention for his "Sky Full of Bacon" series of food documentaries, and served as videographer for the Reader's "Key Ingredient" chef challenge series. He won a James Beard Foundation award for the latter, and has been nominated two other times for his videos. He launched Fooditor in 2015.

Overleaf: Furious Spoon

Made in the USA
Lexington, KY
07 December 2016